Big God

Everyday Miracles

The journey continues

Debrah J Smith

Copyright © Debrah J Smith 2022 All rights re
served. This book or parts thereof may not be
 reproduced in any form, stored in any retrieval
system, or transmitted in any form by any means—
electronic, mechanical, photocopy, recording, or
otherwise—without prior written permission of the
publisher, except as provided by United States of
America copyright law. For permission requests,
write to the publisher, at "Attention: Permissions
Coordinator," at the address below.
ISBN 9781954626041
Independently Published
Debrah J Smith
4251 E Lakeview Dr.
Martinsville, In 46151
Website
www.gloryrealmministries.org
Facebook
www.facebook.com/debrahmeltonsmith
Scripture taken from the New King James Bible, ©
1979, 1980, 1983, 1985, Thomas Nelson Used by
permission. Unless otherwise noted.
NLT © 1996,2004,2015 Tyndale House Founda-
tion
Cover illustration by Kenneth M Smith

CONTENTS

Chapter One- Divine Appointment

Chapter Two- Church In The Streets

Chapter Three- It's The Little Things

Chapter Four- Light In The Darkness

Chapter Five- Let The Worshipers Arise

Chapter Six- The Favor Of The Lord

Chapter Seven- First Peace Then Power

Chapter Eight- The Year Of Turmoil And Power

Chapter Nine- A New Name

Chapter Ten- Let Your Yes Be Yes

Chapter Eleven- Not Many Fathers

Chapter Twelve- Open Portals

Chapter Thirteen- Victory In The Wait

Chapter Fourteen- Be Ready

Chapter Fifteen- Open Doors

Chapter Sixteen- God Turns Negative Into Positive

Chapter Seventeen- Speak The Truth

Chapter Eighteen- Prayer Room Results

Chapter Nineteen- Prayer Room Update

Chapter Twenty- Changing a Culture

Chapter Twenty-One- The Bride

CHAPTER ONE

4-30-21: Divine Appointment

Today was an ordinary day with extraordinary endings! We were invited to go out boating with some old and some new friends. We were introduced to the new friends by the owners of the boat and enjoyed all of their company for the day! We had been wanting to enjoy some island hopping but without a boat of our own, that wasn't happening but God provided the opportunity.

Later in the day we went on a bike ride to check out an AirBNB for our son. He may come down to Florida next winter and places get snatched up quickly so I told him I'd check out the area for him now. I saw a small group of three ladies sitting outside on their patio which was right in front of the property that I was looking at for my son. I said "excuse me, can I ask you a question?" They said "yes" so I got off my bike and walked over to where they were sitting. I asked them about the neighborhood and whether it was safe and quiet. They all agreed that my son would be happy there.

By that time I had built a rapport with the ladies. They had introduced themselves. Race does not matter to me at all but I was not sure how they'd feel about me being white, one of the ladies was a kind black lady. Those that know me also know that I'm an introvert by nature but when God has a plan, things flow so beautifully. After talking for a while, I asked them If they went to church anywhere. The Black lady said a resounding Yes! There was an empty chair and I asked if I could sit, all the while not realizing that I was there for a greater purpose. I told them where I went to church and how we landed there. I started telling them the story and my husband, the social butterfly, got off his bike to come over as well. He's usually the one doing the talking and was probably coming to help me out but I said "let me tell them my story." I told them how we ended up at our church (The Well) at just the right time.

I shared that my husband, daughter in law, grand-daughter, and I got COVID the first two weeks of our stay here in Florida. After going through the two weeks of loss of smell, loss of taste, and EX-TREME fatigue, I was so ready to go to church! We had been so sick that our son, the only one who didn't get sick, brought us soup daily and checked on us while we lay on the couches, unable to even get dressed! So once again, I was ready to get up, get dressed, put make-up on, and go! We were both very weak but I knew if I could just get into the corporate atmosphere of worship I would be strengthened! I told my husband that we must go to the church down the street from us. We had visited there before and felt God's presence in the house! To be continued!

Today is September 11th and many things have happened since this encounter, in April! I never finished the story because of a mental blockage, of sort, to write. That dam has been broken and the words of the Lord have been revealed to me to carry on! I went to a "Beloved Warrior day away" this morning with my daughter Kindel and she led the worship for the event. I was inspired, in God's presence, to stop burying my gifts! He reminded me of my heart (vision) to Minister to women out of my own life experiences and to give hope to those that are weary! It wasn't until I got home, and began mowing my yard, that the Lord gave me the title of this new book. "Big God Everyday Miracles"

More on that later but I must finish the previous story! I don't want to leave you hanging!
April 30th- I'll pick up where I left off in my story. We went to church that morning in mid December,

at the end of our 2 week quarantine and God met us there! I told my husband,on the way to church, that I felt different both physically and spiritually. I also said "I feel like God is taking me to a new place in Him!" Because of the loss of taste and smell and no appetite, I had lost 10 pounds but while I lost weight I gained much more spiritually! I became so hungry for my Lord that I had been changed from the inside out. During the time on the couch where I was forced to be at rest, Jesus met me there! We were saturating ourselves with Worship and the Word and spiritual hunger caused us to draw nearer to Jesus! During this time, I was asking God "why did we and our family get this horrible sickness"? I had prayed and covered all of us, and all my church families as well, with the blood of the lamb! I never doubted His powers, just myself! I even wondered, during this time of hopelessness, if He heard my prayers! Well let me tell you, I got my answer that morning!

We were greeted by Janet and Doug at the door of the church and their welcome melted my heart! I was done with the isolation and needed fellowship with other believers. I walked through the doors of the sanctuary and immediately began to weep in His presence! Service hadn't started yet but I was ready to enter into the Holy place of His presence! During the worship time the pastor called families up to front for prayer and we both went. Almost the whole congregation lined up for prayer and the Pastor was clear at the other end of the line but came back to us to start ministry.

He gave my husband a word from the Lord and then it was my turn. I wasn't expecting that at all since I just wanted to bask in His presence! He stopped and pondered for a minute and said, "you've got a place that you go to pray and you wonder if He hears you, He does!" The backstory is that I have a prayer room both in Florida and Indiana! Tears came again and he said, "you're coming into a new season in Him!" I related this entire story to these ladies and the kind black lady, Diane, asked me to join a Bible study she was having every Thursday and I accepted with joy. You see I had another request of Jesus, during that time! I asked Him for opportunities to minister and He provided! I only had two more weeks in Florida but both Thursdays mornings were spent with Diane and Gwendolyn! Rich conversation around the Word of God was fulfilling for the three of us. I can't wait to get back there and do it again but once again the Lord has given me "provision for the vision". Open doors of opportunity have opened this day, May 11th 2021, a day we will always remember! He takes all things and turns them for good! He's heard my prayers and my longings to share the goodness of God with a hopeless generation!

CHAPTER TWO

5-23-21: Church In The Streets

My husband and I had planned a camping trip to Madison, Indiana for the weekend. We brought our new ebikes to try out on the beautiful trail along the river. As a backstory, I would add that I had been feeling a little discouraged that my life was not making an impact. I wanted to share Jesus but I'm not as outspoken as my husband so I had judged myself. So here we are, minding our own business, when Jesus is about to give us a divine appointment! So on with the story.

There are lovely flower beds and benches along the path that invite a peaceful resting place. This reminds me of Jesus! And, by the way, part of this path was once a railroad track with the old tracks still there. The Lord just gave me this amazing scripture that speaks exactly to where I found myself along this beautiful Ohio river path!

"He offers a resting place for me in his luxurious love. His tracks take me to an oasis of peace near the quiet brook of bliss. That's where he restores and revives my life. He opens before me the right path and leads me along in his footsteps of righteousness so that I can bring honor to his name." Psalms 23:2-3 TPT

So we were just enjoying the evening ride, here at the end of the trail, and saw the opportunity to sit down and rest. As I walked my bike over to sit, I saw a small very old book propped up on the bench as if beaconing me to pick it up! I couldn't resist so I sat down with my husband and looked it over. The title was "CHILD STORY READERS" with a copyright of 1927. There was a bookmark in one of the pages which said FAITH at the top and the signature at the bottom was "Sandra Kuck". It had a little girl walking on the beach showing her footprints and a few shells. The back revealed the footprints poem as follows.

The LORD said,

"My son, my precious child,
I love you and I would never leave you.
During your times of trial and suffering,
When you see only one set of footprints,
It was then that I carried you."

"Be strong and of good courage, do not fear nor be afraid of them; for the Lord your God, He is the One who goes with you. He will not leave you nor forsake you."
Deuteronomy 31:6 NKJV

I was troubled by someone's imminent loss and felt compelled to find the owner! It was supposed to rain later that evening and I couldn't bear to allow the book to be ruined. The lighting was bad and I didn't have my reading glasses so when I looked at the bookmark the signature appeared to belong to the actual owner of the book; At least in my mind! The next day revealed it to be digitally embossed on the marker and not the signature of the book owner but the designer of the marker. I know this seems tedious but there's a reason to share this as you will soon learn. God uses the unusual to express the miraculous!

We sat there, for a while, wondering what to do. When a couple walked up the path. I immediately asked them if they knew "Sandra Kuck" since I assumed they were local. They were on an anniversary weekend but lived on the other side of the Ohio River in Kentucky. I told them about the book and we connected as fellow believers. We spoke of angels and divine appointments. They were pastors and he worked construction so Ken, my husband, related to that! We shared testimonies and had a great time!

A few minutes later, a family (mom, dad, several teens, and a dog) piled out of a truck and a Harley right there where we were talking. I asked them if they knew "Sandra" and I have to laugh now but God knew what He was doing! They looked a little rough with many tattoos and piercings. Dad was a large man that looked scary as he dismounted his Harley. We introduced them to our new friends and the man began to share his story!

He had just gotten out of prison, just a short time before this divine appointment, after several years incarcerated. He then proceeded to tell us that he got saved and used his entire prison time to study the Bible, pray for inmates, studied the Bible in Hebrew, and turned his life completely around! This was one of the first times that he was able to share what God had done for him and he was so blessed by this encounter as well!

By the time we were done talking, Jesus had orchestrated "church on the streets" out of finding a small book left there by an unknown person! We left the book and went back to the RV hoping that someone would retrieve it. Right before the rain was supposed to start, I asked Ken if we could check on the book that "Jesus" left. He was not too thrilled to get back out and ride in the dark but he saw I was intent on it and agreed. It was still there, I picked it up, we rode back a mile, and the rain started. Just remember "never judge a BOOK by its cover" Lord help me to remember that and also to trust You to use me to reveal You! The book is a reminder of the little things that often go unnoticed!

CHAPTER THREE

12-5-21: It's Just The Little Things

I woke up this morning and had an awesome time just singing my worship to Jesus! I entered into a time of all out surrender to Him! It was so beautiful that I wanted to stay in that place with Him. I had been feeling somewhat disconnected because I hadn't really gone this deep in awhile but He was there just waiting to meet with me! I've been in a place unable to write, as He requested, and I felt uninspired and inadequate. He was about to rock my world with another LITTLE miracle!

It was a Sunday morning and I wanted to attend the prayer time early at our church in Indiana. Ken was already gone as he was filling in on the worship team so my Jesus time was uninterrupted but now it was time to go. I went out to the car to start it as it had been colder than usual and I noticed that the seat heater light was on! I had not turned it on since we've tried numerous times and the light would go on and immediately turn off without heating up. This has been the case since we bought this used car several years ago. We've prayed, many times, that the heater would work but to no apparent avail! The passenger side always worked but not the driver's side and this is the car I drive! I began to cry as I felt the seat warm underneath me! I kept watching, with amazement, as the light burned brightly and my body felt not only physical warmth but the warmth of His great love for me! I could hardly contain my excitement for this special gift!

"Always be joyful. Never stop praying. Be thankful in all circumstances, for this is God's will for you who belong to Christ Jesus."
1 Thessalonians 5:16-18 NLT
James 5:16 fervent prayer avails much, Matt. 6:33 seek first

CHAPTER FOUR

12-16-2021- Light In The Darkness

This morning my Devotional spoke of the great "I Am" and the light that He brings! His first "I Am" statement is in the book of John, "I Am the bread of life", which he spoke after feeding the five thousand and this is the second.
There is so much darkness all around us. Where do we find light? The answer to that is in Jesus' second "I Am" statement. He said: "I am the light of the world." The world was dark when Jesus was on earth too. Ever since sin first entered the world through Adam and Eve, the world has been full of darkness.

I had a dream early this morning that spoke of that light! I was at a mall of sorts with some other ladies and I left them to explore, by myself, on an outside trail leading to a place I hadn't been and didn't know where it ended. I walked on a muddy, icy, treacherous road filled with potholes which speaks of the hard and narrow road that leads to the true light.

"Enter by the narrow gate; for wide is the gate and broad is the way that leads to destruction, and there are many who go in by it. Because narrow is the gate and difficult is the way which leads to life, and there are few who find it."
Matthew 7:13-14 NKJV

I came across a play area that had a fort-like structure, like what we might see at the many state parks we've camped in, and a bunch of young people were gathered there! I felt very bold (not usual for me), and walked up to them to ask If they knew my Jesus. They didn't really respond but lingered around me wanting to hear more! A few of the young guys were flirting with me. The Lord showed me this morning that they were attracted to Jesus in me, not in some perverted way.

There were preteens there as well that were longing for a connection with me, again Jesus! I asked if they wanted to hear a worship song and sing along. As I sang and looked around, I noticed a beautiful waterfall that brought peace although it was out of place for where I was. So I'm laughing now as I write this as the Lord prompted me to look up the word waterfall and what He showed me ignited in the middle of sharing this dream. Wow and again He shows up! The word ignited was an auto correct for my rendering of right. He has ignited me right in the middle of this sharing so I won't correct the "MISTAKE"!

"Deep calls unto deep at the noise of Your waterfalls; All Your waves and billows have gone over me. The Lord will command His loving kindness in the daytime, And in the night His song shall be with me— A prayer to the God of my life."
Psalms 42:7-8 NKJV

Back to the dream but not sorry as I was interrupted to listen and hear from my Heavenly Father! I'm noticing that as I'm sharing the dream that the Lord is further revealing it's deeper meaning! This is a part of the daily miracles that we sometimes ignore.

I stayed so long that it had gotten "dark" and I told them my "friends" were waiting for me at the mall.

"And everyone who has given up houses or brothers or sisters or father or mother or children or property, for my sake, will receive a hundred times as much in return and will inherit eternal life."
Matthew 19:29 NLT

"Jesus asked, "Who is my mother? Who are my

brothers?" Anyone who does the will of my Father in heaven is my brother and sister and mother!""
Matthew 12:48, 50 NLT

I had no phone, to call my friends, or a flashlight to find my way back as I was walking and didn't even know where I was. He knew exactly where I was and what was to be accomplished there as He is the LIGHT of the world. I felt compelled to stay longer as they were begging me not to leave them!

One child sat on my lap hugging me tight while tears flowed from her eyes. They found a candle and lit it for me as I finally had to go! There were many tears as they longed for what I had shared with them! I'm so thankful that Jesus never leaves us and gives us a command to be strong, coura-geous, and not afraid.

"Jesus replied, "Are there not twelve hours of day-light every day? You can go through a day without the fear of stumbling when you walk in the One who gives light to the world. But you will stumble when the light is not in you, for you'll be walking in the dark."
John 11:9-10 TPT

These young people seem to be waiting in the "dark" for someone to show them the TRUE light! He has shown me that our young, and old as well, are so hungry for the "REAL JESUS" that we carry! He speaks to us daily if we pay attention to dreams, devotionals, and all the little miracles that happen every day! We are the light and our love and compassion will dispel the darkness and bring hope to the hungry ones! This "short" sharing of a dream has become a two and a half hour experience with my Jesus! He knew that I needed inspiration to write more about Him and His every day miracles and He has richly provided! Thank you Jesus for the dream and more revelation of who you are to ALL of us!

CHAPTER FIVE

12-21-21: Let The Worshipers Arise

This morning I was awoken by a dream that startled me out of sleep! I was in the lobby at church as there was a beautiful worship program being set up. There were many true worshipers involved but, out of nowhere, they all came out of the sanctuary doors visibly shaken! They had ALL been replaced by professional well known performers! I was so grieved by this that I was literally on my face crying out to God!

My face was on the carpet with tears wet beneath me. It was like a purging out of true heart worship for a plastic like performance oriented imitation! I'm still grieved in my spirit as I recall the dream as it seemed real yet alarming! I believe that the Lord gives us these warnings in our most vulnerable times like in sleep. This has happened to me many times and I tend to pay attention especially when I can't get them out of my head.

Many times we are so busy, during our waking hours, that we fail to spend the time needed to listen. This is a picture of what has happened in many houses of worship. Jesus is looking for the true worshipers that worship in Spirit and in truth! Lord speak, as your servant listens! So I was just impressed to write the previous words and then realized that's a scripture! Just wow!

"So he said to Samuel, "Go and lie down again, and if someone calls again, say, 'Speak, Lord, your servant is listening.'" So Samuel went back to bed."
1 Samuel 3:9 NLT

CHAPTER SIX

1-8-22: The Favor Of The Lord

Today I have several nuggets of favor that I need to share!

We have been clearing out our back yard of debris left after the cutting down and trimming of several trees. Ken's electric pole saw was being used beyond its capacity which resulted in the chain in need of either a sharpening or perhaps a new blade! As he continued working, I said that I would take it to Ace hardware for whatever they could do for it. I was excited to see him doing this work so I offered to make the run with my motives being, I wanted the work to continue! Lol!

The man at the repair desk got out his papers and started to take my information for the saw to be sent out to be sharpened. They don't do it there so I asked about just getting a new blade since we needed it TODAY, again my longing for this job to be completed! He said, "let me look". He came back kind of surprised looking and said, "wow this is the ONLY one that will fit and it's the last one!

This was a unique saw with hard to find parts. He handed me the chain in the package and I said "what am I supposed to do with this now?" It was kind of funny as I stood there wide-eyed holding the chain as he said, "take it to the register to pay!" He said, doesn't your guy know how to put it on?" I said, "I don't know!" He said, "give it here" in a frustrating but kind way and off he went to the back of the store. By the way, they weren't busy at all, especially for a Saturday afternoon!

He came back and handed it to me and I just needed to pay for the chain! I was so excited about this gift from my Father and couldn't wait to tell Ken. I came back with a smile on my face that wasn't going to last too long. As soon as he took one pass through our jungle, the chain came off again and he couldn't put the thing back together!

I know this seems long but joy does come in the morning, literally. We called around for repair places and they were all closed until Monday. We called Monday and every place we called said that they didn't work on electric saws, UNTIL someone suggested a place not advertised! We called the place and they told us to bring it in and they would see what they could do. Ken took it and was gone a long time so I was wondering what was going on with the saw that Jesus blessed! So, once again, the store was not busy and a young employee took a look. The guys put their heads together and put the saw back together as well!

Ken tried to pay the guy but he wouldn't take money. I believe he received more than money can buy in that interaction. I love when Jesus gives us these divine appointments as I'm confident that HE was brought up somewhere in the conversation!

"Two people are better off than one, for they can help each other succeed."
Ecclesiastes 4:9 NLT

CHAPTER SEVEN

1-16-22- First Peace than Power

This morning I was awoken by a loud alarm on Ken's phone, he had fallen asleep with it in the bed. I thought it was an amber alert but it was a tornado warning! I got up and it was 5:30am. And the winds were literally howling at close to 50mph.

My son and his wife were leaving Tarpon to travel to his Dad's house, nearly three hours away. They were set to leave at 7am and I texted him to let him know of the winds and heavy rain. I told him to be careful on the road and that I was praying. Then a couple minutes later I said, "consider waiting". I laid back down but was still concerned for their safety so I began to pray in tongues!

All of a sudden, the wind and rain stopped completely. This was just minutes before they were set to leave! I sent him one more text that said, Thank

you Lord! Peace be still! He said, thinking I was still concerned, "Go back to sleep". I did and Jesus had already answered this Momma's prayer!
I was able to rest in Him and be ready for the day as if no sleep was lost!

1-16-22 Later in the day

This is still the same day and The Lord has continued to download me. It started with a Devotional I'm reading with my 15 year old Granddaughter, her choice of study. It talked about being connected with God! They referred to the teen's IPhone being charged and all the potential of reaching friends, Snap, Instagram as well as asking Siri questions and all its endless possibilities.

 If it's not charged (plugged in) then it's useless even though the potential is there for more! I read the Devotional but it didn't have the impact until several hours later in a worship service!

 I was just minding my own business, in worship, when the Lord dropped this thought in my mind. There's two kinds of electricity that we can connect to,110 volt and 220 volt. I decided to pray into that thought and do some research since I'm not an electrician. What are YOU saying to me today Lord?

My first thought is that I would choose to be a 220v Christian so we'll see how that works out for me as I research.

"Never doubt God's mighty power to work in you and accomplish all this. He will achieve infinitely more than your greatest request, your most unbelievable dream, and exceed your wildest imagination! He will outdo them all, for his miraculous power constantly energizes you."
Ephesians 3:20 TPT

This reminds me of the energizer bunny, it keeps going and going! His power never stops!

The 220v line is more efficient in terms of current (Holy Spirit Power) so the greater the openness of the vessel, the greater the power that flows through. The 220v poses a higher RISK and requires more safety protocols when installing or repairing! In layman's terms 220v is more efficient but comes with more of a RISK as well a greater COST upfront!

Wiring that is heavier duty is also more expensive to purchase. Appliances such as dryers, stoves, and water heaters require 220v to power them! They are considered heavy duty when it comes to the power it takes to run them! Some keywords here are RISK, COST, EFFICIENCY, AND POWER!

Sounds scary? Not if you're connected (plugged in) to the power of the Holy Spirit! The cost was paid for by Jesus at the cross but it will cost us our lives submitted to Him to have the fullness of His Spirit!

We need to be fully plugged into the correct outlets in order to work effectively. The 220 outlets have a special outlet that can only be accessed with the correct plug! His 220 Power can only be assessed with our lives full of His Spirit. Have you ever tried to plug a cord into an outlet and it just won't fit? We need the wisdom of God to get plugged into the right place at the right time!

Sometimes, the cost may seem too high when friends or family leave you because of the Power that dwells within you. What about when you are drawn to witness to those same ones? The RISK is worth the REWARD! I believe that risk is synonymous with faith in these situations! Are we willing to risk rejection and see the reward of a life changed for the gospel?

More on the technical part of the operation: With the current level fixed in a home, the volts (prayers) must be increased in order to provide that power, which is where 220v wiring provides the needed boost. Also, 220v power is more efficient (effective) in terms of current because it requires

26

less to provide the same power due to the increased voltage. As mentioned previously, however, this increase also means 220v poses a higher safety risk than 110v.

Our voltage of prayer must increase if we are to see the power (220v Holy Ghost) we desire but we will also experience resistance from the enemy! It may seem dangerous to live all out for God because of this but He promises that we can dwell in safety! (Psalm 4:8.)

What about the ordinary, everyday 110 outlet that we use to plug in our lamps? The lamp is low wattage and doesn't take much power to operate it but it also doesn't put out the powerful rays of your neighborhood street light. The 110 outlet is safe, there's very little risk, repairs are usually inexpensive, and it requires less skill and knowledge to do so. There's little power that is needed to operate in that realm.

I'm wondering, as I write this, which one of these outlets would you like to be or should I say which plug? Would you choose the 220 of the Holy Spirit with all the risk, reward, danger, and effectiveness, or the 110 which is easy, virtually safe, risk free, but little power. Another thought, the outlet for the 220 CAN NOT be accessed by a 110 plug!

We traveled to England where the outlets AP-
PEARED to be the same as our 110 here but we're
actually 220. We plugged in a new NutriBullet
and burnt it up even though we used a US to UK
converter. The converter was fake news! We can't
be fake when it comes to our relationship with the
Father, Son and Holy Spirit. The power in the outlet was GREATER than the plug! The power in us
(our plug) must match up to the powerful outlet of
the Holy Spirit! Reading this now for editing and
I'm wowed by His amazing ability to speak to us
in unusual ways!

CHAPTER EIGHT

1-24- 2022: A Year of Turmoil And Power

This morning I have an opportunity to spend some time with Jesus while my husband goes to the gym. Since my husband and I are together all the time, this is a special time for me to seek God in the secret place of His presence! I started reading my Bible, for inspiration, and I saw a scripture in Romans 3 that I underlined.

"His gift of love and favor now cascades over us, all because Jesus, the Anointed One, has liberated us from the guilt, punishment, and power of sin!"

Romans 3:24b TPT

It goes on to say in verse 25, that He is our mercy seat because of His death on the cross! The mercy seat was the lid to the ark of the covenant which was carried in the wilderness and then finally found its home in the temple in Jerusalem. Only the priests went in privately, every year, to the holy place to sprinkle blood on the "mercy seat" for the sins of the people. Jesus was publicly offered up and His blood shed thereby becoming OUR mercy seat in heaven!

So I was thinking about all this, His favor, His love, His mercy then I asked Him a question. This topic of love, favor, mercy and I'll add justice, reminded me of a word He had given me for 2022 back in late December 2021 regarding our upcoming state of affairs. I had asked Him to give me a heads up of what was on the horizon for us as a nation.

The word was turmoil!
A state of great disturbance, confusion, or uncertainty. "The country was in turmoil" This is the dictionary's rendering!

I asked Him to show me further what this meant beyond what that definition implied! He said, War in the Heavenlies" which is actually a good thing for us! Some people are speaking out about a great future with everything settling down and things getting better and back to "normal" but this was NOT the word that was given to me! I hesitated sharing, but now I must based on the "War in the Heavenlies" that is coming!

"Then a terrible war broke out in heaven. Michael and his
Angels fought against the great dragon. The dragon and his angels fought back. But the dragon did not have the power to win and they could not regain their place in heaven. So the great dragon was thrown down once and for all. He was the serpent, the ancient snake called the devil, and Satan, who deceives the whole earth. He was cast down into the earth and his angels along with him. Then I heard a triumphant voice in heaven proclaiming: "Now salvation and power are set in place, and the kingdom reign of our God and the ruling authority of his Anointed One are established. For the accuser of our brothers and sisters, who relentlessly accused them day and night before our God, has now been defeated—cast out once and for all! They conquered him completely through the blood of the Lamb and the powerful word of his testimony. They triumphed because they did not love and cling to their own lives, even when faced with death. So rejoice, you heavens, and every heavenly being! But woe to the earth and the sea, for the devil has come down to you with great fury, because he knows his time is short."
Revelation 12:7-12 TPT

We may be in a state of great uncertainty along with confusion, but He's the author of peace! God is still in control. If we allow Him to be our Lord

He will calm the storms and bring us through the chaos and turmoil! Satan has been defeated and IS being defeated! Take heart my friends, the King is coming!

33

CHAPTER NINE

1-30-22: A New Name

So this morning as we were in church worshiping our Lord, a young man asked my husband if he could sit with us! Of course, he said yes! I didn't see him right away since I had my eyes closed in a zone with Jesus! When I did see him, as worship was over, I was struck by how much he reminded me of our oldest grandson! His manner of dress, haircut and color, and demeanor all said Luke!

The sermon along with some prophetic words sung during worship referred to us receiving a "new name"!

Our name is not "unworthy" "unloved" "ashamed" "guilty" but quite different! Our new names are "righteous", "forgiven", "worthy", and "loved"! This is all claimed through the blood of Jesus as we accept Him as our beloved Savior!
"The nations will see your righteousness. World

leaders will be blinded by your glory. And you will be given a new name by the Lord's own mouth." Isaiah 62:2 NLT

So going back to the young man, I whispered to My husband, "doesn't he look like Luke"? This was at the end of the service and my husband said, "yeah say something to him!" Well anyone who knows me and Ken knows that he is the one that always has something to say but not me as much!

I was compelled to speak with him so I went over and introduced myself and asked for his name. His name was David! I knew, right then, that I needed to tell him about my name change that happened to me more than thirty years previous. As I listened to the words spoken and sung that morning, it reminded me of this monumental event in my life! I've written about it in a previous book "Pearls of Wisdom",but will revisit it here.

I told him that I had been named Debrah at birth but everyone, except one of my aunts, called me Debbie! This aunt saw more in me than I did myself! I had been saved, quite a while by this time, and this would be my second name change since I had already received my new name of "forgiven".

Debbie was the little girl that was broken, hurt,

weak, and insecure! Jesus told me audibly, "you are as your name". I began to research "Deborah" in the Bible and learned that she was a very strong woman of God! She was a judge, she led armies when the men were not willing to, she was a prophetess, songwriter, and she was also the wife of Lappidoth or lappid which translates as "torch" or "lightning"! She was a fiery woman!

Now I didn't share all of that, at this quick exchange, but enough to make a point that we are not named by accident or chance! I also shared my daughter's name, "Kindel", as she kindles the flames of worship in our church back in Indiana as the worship leader. This is when I reminded him of his name David, that was no coincidence! David was a crazy worshiper so much that he danced his clothes off while his wife watched in disgust!

 He told us that his Dad had another name picked but his Mom insisted on David! We both spoke into his life and his name! He maybe has not seen it all at this point but he will! I know that we met him for a reason! He asked if we were coming next week and we said, yes! This was his first time here! To be continued!

1-31-22 NEXT DAY

This morning, Ken and I were working on putting up a new fence along our back yard which backs up to the Pinellas bike trail. I happened to be out there holding a board for him while facing the trail when I saw David riding fast past our house! I almost dropped the heavy board on our toes!

 I yelled really loud and I saw him turn his head a bit but kept going! We didn't have David's last name or contact info and I was a little distressed thinking, we may not be able to follow up with him! No coincidences with Jesus, He'll make a way!

CHAPTER TEN

2-6-22: Let Your Yes Be Yes

Today we are going to join Mario Murillo in a tent meeting in Naples Florida and we were going to either not go to church or leave early as we have a three hour trip to get there in time for the meeting.

I really wanted to enjoy the warmth and beauty of this town before the meeting started. I felt compelled to go to church because we told David we would be there and we had no way to contact him!

Let your yes be yes and your no be no. Matt.5:37 We went and I didn't see David at first but he did arrive a little later! I told the Lord that I would stay however long it took to minister to him in whatever way that He needed!

I had the opportunity to be an altar worker that morning and be available to anyone needing prayer! I was hoping that David would go up for prayer but he didn't. After church I asked him if I could pray for him and he agreed! I am so glad that I put my wants aside for this time! We got his contact info and we both gave him hugs! We can't allow ourselves to be self absorbed when there's people that need what we have, His Presence! We told him that we would see him next week and invited him to bike ride us sometime soon!

CHAPTER ELEVEN

2-13-22: Not Many Fathers

FYI David was there and once again God had a divine encounter ready for him through my husband Ken this time! Ken was able to speak to him as a father and encourage him in his walk with the Lord. The young man revealed that he had an estranged relationship with his father. The Lord has provided Ken with a son to mentor and given David a Father figure to encourage him in his walk. We are so blessed to be used in touching others with His amazing love and goodness! Don't take lightly the people that He puts in front of you! Don't be too busy to love, engage, encourage, and bless those that He puts in your path! No coincidences, only divine appointments! This world needs fathers and mothers in the faith to help guide this generation to Jesus!

CHAPTER TWELVE

2-14-22: Open Portals

This morning Ken got a message from some friends in Indiana and they were asking us to come and lead worship for a ministry here in Florida. They had just moved to an area south of us, three weeks previously, and we didn't know that as we had lost touch with them.

They got connected with the "Courtside Ministry", here in Florida, and they were asking us to lead them in a time of worship for their upcoming regional gathering. We had been a part of this ministry in our hometown of Martinsville, In but didn't realize this was nationwide!

She said her husband had been following my husband Ken on Facebook and saw that we were doing several weekly outreaches. We committed to worship Jesus at our local beach every Wednesday night at sunset as well as some Clearwater beach outreaches on random Saturday nights. We were called to be outside the four walls to where people could be found that so need a refreshing touch from Jesus! Again, we have been asking the Lord to open the doors of ministry while we continue to do all we know to do.

No one invited us to the beach, we just went and put action to our faith.
You never know who is watching you and how The Lord will work behind the scenes to make you known to them.

The Lord has shown me, this year, to know and be known! I've gotten involved in prayer and women's Bible study at our church here in Florida so I can KNOW them and they can KNOW me and I'm talking about Spiritually. We are known by the fruits of the Spirit working in our lives! Remember our roots produce our fruits!

"But the fruit produced by the Holy Spirit within you is divine love in all its varied expressions: joy that overflows, peace that subdues, patience that endures, kindness in action, a life full of virtue, faith that prevails, gentleness of heart, and strength of spirit. Never set the law above these qualities, for they are meant to be limitless."
Galatians 5:22-23 TPT

I love this version that says it so well, all the fruits express love! Lord help us all to be aware of our fruits be it yummy or rotten! More updates on this event as the date draws near.

CHAPTER TWELVE

2-15-22 :Victory In the Wait

I was thinking about how as we wait on the Lord for answers to prayers, He is working behind the scenes to bring it to fruition! We've asked the Lord for open doors of opportunities to share His love, the faith that He's given us, hope to a hopeless generation, and just an All out trust in an unfailing God!

And guess what, He's doing it but we've had to wait! Waiting is not popular in this microwave, instapot, air fryer kinda world! Don't get me wrong I like those items as well but there are times when the WAIT is necessary!

"But those who wait on the Lord Shall renew their strength; They shall mount up with wings like eagles, They shall run and not be weary, They shall walk and not faint."
Isaiah 40:31 NKJV

The Lord showed me, just now, that we get STRONGER in the WAIT! You might be in the waiting room or maybe just in the hallway but your time is coming to see the manifestations of the WAIT!

I feel so incredibly grateful just like a Mother after the birth of her long awaited child. She's waited nine months and then comes the result of her wait, a precious gift from heaven. She forgets the struggle of the wait and even the pain that has transpired for the joy that has come as a result of the WAIT!

I am more in love with the lover of my soul as I rehearse the years of faithfulness! In the waiting is the time to remember the many small everyday Miracles that we can dismiss if we're not aware of His presence! We still have not seen the whole of what He wants to do with us but today I'm thankful for the WAIT as I burn! Whoa God! Typo for burn as I tried to write churn twice! Allow the churn to happen! Churn- to stir or agitate violently then comes the BURN!

"Here's what I've learned through it all: Don't give up; don't be impatient; be entwined as one with the Lord. Be brave and courageous, and never lose hope. Yes, keep on waiting—for he will never disappoint you!"
Psalms 27:14 TPT

CHAPTER FOURTEEN

2-22-22: Be Ready

This morning I was awoken by an interesting dream and I didn't really see the significance until I was reading Matthew 24 concerning the end times. Then I turned to the next chapter 25, recalling the story of the ten virgins.

The dream: I was going to a birthday party (celebration of life) and I had no card or gift so I decided to make a cake! I put the cake in the pan and quickly iced it very beautifully and realized that I had not BAKED the cake! I was thinking that maybe I could still salvage it by baking it that way but it didn't work!

I'm thinking how can you put icing on a cake that was still wet, you can not! I thought, in my dream, the cake was not READY. I hadn't followed the instructions, in the correct order, because I was so busy with how it would look! Then I woke up! As I read about the ten virgins, the Lord highlighted the dream to me!

My offering, or gift, that I brought was not finished and not ready to be given. I did not follow the instructions given (Bible). I was not ready for the celebration! Five out of the ten virgins were ready to meet the bridegroom and the others were called foolish as they were not ready with plenty of oil for their lamps as they found themselves in the dark of the night.

The bridegroom came in the middle of the night, and in the darkness, the foolish ones weren't ready. They did not plan for this quick and unexpected arrival time. They were not AWAKE to what was coming; the marriage supper was starting as they went to buy oil! The foolish ones were locked out as they pleaded for entrance and the groom said, "I don't even KNOW you!"

They must've regretted their lack of really knowing the Father enough to be AWARE and AWAKE! We need to live our lives as though the Lord will come today even with the darkness all around us as we walk in His light.

I want to be fully READY, full of Holy Spirit oil, when He comes with my lamp burning bright so others will come to the light as well! Thank you Jesus for a great reminder that You are coming soon!

CHAPTER FIFTEEN

3- 12-22: Open Doors

It's been awhile since I've written anything but God has been on the move and at the same time so has the enemy! Guess who's winning? More on that later!

Today is the day of our ministry at the Courtside regional gathering that I spoke of back on February 14th. The weather is awful with very high winds(50mph) with a massive storm coming in! The winds and booming thunder actually woke us up early and I encouraged my husband to get up and load the car before the rains came in. He did and not five minutes later the rains came!

We loaded the car by faith that we were still on for this! I texted our friends to see if there was a plan B since this was to be an outside event on a beautiful beach! We had an hour and a half drive so wanted to make sure it was still on. They did have a clubhouse reserved as well so we were good to go! We were going to stay in the area and enjoy the beautiful beaches there in Bradenton but God had a different plan.

We arrived early and the rain let up a little so we could unload our equipment. We were supposed to eat lunch at noon and then do worship but things changed and we didn't eat until around one. I say this because, the fruit of the Spirit, patience, needed to be in operation as we were way past hungry!

We ended up leading worship at the end instead of the beginning and it was a wonderful time! Believers from many different backgrounds lifted their hands and hearts to Jesus! Sometimes it's hard to go with the flow when things go differently than you expect but resting in Him and allowing Him to lead is really awesome!

I was concerned that we wouldn't be done in time to go to our next assignment, more on that shortly, but we wrapped up in a good place and timely as well. We also found out, from the man that was hosting this event, that they tried to get some worship leaders from their church to do the worship but to no avail. Our Indiana friends offered our names up as a possibility and without knowing us, He said,"yes" please ask them," The Lord was working it out for his plan! We also found out that

Evan, an older gentleman that we work with at the Clearwater outreach, was already involved in this ministry! Evan was there along with our friends/ministry partners Mark and Carrie so we all signed up to start up a new location in Pasco county near us! This was definitely a DIVINE appointment.

Our ministry partners Mark and Carrie rode with us and we thought, since the weather was ugly and we weren't going to stay in the area, we would go to a meeting in Largo on the way back.

John and Carol Arnott were speaking at a small church called "Catch the Fire". They were the Pastors of the Toronto Vineyard Airport revival back in 1994. Ken and I had visited there once while on vacation to Niagara Falls in 1997 and it was quite the experience. The power of God was truly evident so we thought we'd go and check it out!

More patience needed here as the meeting started late! If you know me, I can be very long-suffering but I also like timeliness maybe a little more! Lol The sound system kept feed-backing and screeching as we started late and by now I'm tired!

The enemy was trying to stop the move of God there but the worship leaders pressed into their calling! After the worship was over, John Arnnott and his wife replayed the timeline of the modern

Pentecostal movement and where we are now! God wants us to cultivate a love for Him, that was his message in a nutshell!

The idea of the cross was from the Father to express His love through giving His son! There's a dual sacrifice here. Both experienced pain and suffering! Just these two thoughts will cultivate in us the love needed to touch the world for Him!

Many fear God as a bully in heaven beating them down for every wrong move but the fact that He was willing to offer up His son shows the Father heart of God for US! Thank You Lord for You are always good!

An update is in order here. My husband told me that a man, wheelchair bound, rolled up behind him and started speaking into his ear. This was right before they both went up for prayer. The man's words were "Your time is NOW! You carry fire! You and your wife are remnant fire starters. God needs you! It's now! Now is your time! You are to touch others who will carry the fire!"

"I have come to set the earth on fire, and how I wish it were already ablaze with fiery passion for God! But first I must be immersed into the baptism of God's judgment, and I am consumed with passion as I await its fulfillment. Don't think for a

moment that I came to grant peace and harmony to everyone. No, my arrival will change everything and create hostility among you. From now on, even family members will be divided over me and will choose sides one against another. Fathers will be divided from sons and sons from fathers; mothers will be divided from daughters and daughters from mothers; mothers-in-law will be against brides and brides against mothers-in-law—all because of me."
Luke 12:49-53 TPT

As some of you may have experienced, this is happening now! He has sent this fire not to destroy but to purify and cleanse from sin.

"Dear friends, don't be surprised at the fiery trials you are going through, as if something strange were happening to you."
1 Peter 4:12 NLT

As we go through these fiery trials trusting that Jesus has our backs, we grow in our faith and the cares of this world seem to disappear! This happens when we've gone to the other side of the trial into victory! The next time we are faced with something that seems so insurmountable, we remember previous times with thoughts of peace not fear! Do it again Lord!

CHAPTER SIXTEEN

3- 13-22: God Turns a Negative to Positive

I had referred to God being on the move with some resistance from the enemy, in yesterday's writing, but with a promise of explanation.

The whole week before our ministry I was in a funk! There were some gray rainy days and that didn't help but I didn't realize what was really going on until later.

Without being too transparent or revealing the source I'll just say that I was very hurt by some words and attitudes by a Christian leader. I shared something that I felt was happening in a group and It was basically dismissed as not true! I was discerning some things and the person didn't like it and wouldn't even consider it valid. I heard words that devalued me as a person and I felt judged with some other jabs as well. I'm being careful not to be too specific.

So here comes Sunday, and even after the wonderful time we had at the conference, I was still gun-shy to take my place as an altar worker!

The Pastor usually calls us up to pray for folks at the end of service. This week he prayed a group prayer so I thought that I would not be called upon but I was! I decided it was more important to be obedient to Jesus than my own insecurities so I went up! Mind you I've done this several weeks in a row without ANYONE coming my way for prayer!

Backing up for a minute for IMPORTANT background information. When we came into church we put our stuff on our usual chairs and went to have our coffee and bagels in the foyer. We usually leave a spot for David, remember him? Still reaching out and loving him! When we came back in there were a couple nice looking black boys sitting at the end of OUR row! During greeting time, I went over to them and shook their hands and welcomed them. Their mom was sitting behind them and I went to her and asked if she hugged and she answered in the affirmative so I gave her a good hug! I had never seen them before but God had a plan!

Going back to my story as I wipe the tears from my eyes remembering this encounter. I went up front and worshiped God while trying to still be aware if anyone had come up. I opened my eyes and there they were. The mom and her two teenage boys! She requested prayers for them in their school situation but I prayed for more than that as the Holy Spirit led! We were standing in a circle and they moved closer in as I prayed! I embraced them in that circle and told them they were accepted, welcome, and loved by Jesus and me! As the prayer was finished and no one was left in the room but us, the first boy hugged his mom then his brother and then they all hugged and walked away wiping their happy grateful tears! Then I immediately knew why I had gone through this week from the pits. The enemy was trying to stop me from being who God had created me to be! When we are discouraged and about to quit our calling, He is able to help us press through to victory if we will just trust and obey for there's no other way! Remember this, The caller (Jesus) is also the keeper!

CHAPTER SEVENTEEN

3-20-22 : Speak the Truth

I had to come back here and give another testimony of the goodness of God! Once again he's been faithful to send those in need to connect with one who is willing to believe with them.

The two boys from last week came back and came up again for prayer without their Mom this time! They were so precious and my heart was full of love as I shared with them a story of my daughter's purity before marriage. They didn't ask for prayer for this but I felt led to share it and only God knows why!

Kindel, my daughter, was made fun of for her stand of purity in high school as well as at her job. She was mocked and called strawberry and not in a kind way. I encouraged her to stay strong and one day it would pay off. It wasn't long before the same people that mocked her had come to respect her for her standing for what she believed was right. The two boys looked at each other while I was speaking and I could tell that there was a reason I was sharing this! I encouraged them to stand strong for Jesus and their convictions and it would turn out well.

This same day there was another young lady visiting for the first time and we were introduced at the end of the service. She had tears as I embraced her and prayed.
 I had noticed her across the aisle during service and knew that I needed to pray for her. I could tell that the Holy Spirit was touching the very areas that needed to be touched and healed.
 I shared with her about a testimony I had heard from Mellisa Hellser concerning the song "Catch the Wind". The Lord told Mellissa to sing her way out of her pain and the song came out of that experience! I shared the testimony and song link with her and this is what she sent back to me.

"I can't wait to listen! It was so nice meeting you today. I am busy getting dinner to kids and everything right now. But, I would like to share with you what brought me and how you touched me today. I can't thank you enough."

I'm not sharing this for any glory to me but to glorify our wonderful Father with His amazing love for us all! I'm still waiting to hear back what the Lord has done in her and for her but I'm confident that it is good! Everyone can and will be used by God if we are willing, obedient, and aware of those around us! There are hurting people everywhere that need what we have, especially now as the world has gone crazy. We can have such peace in the middle of this storm as we do like Jesus did in His storm and take a nap!

"Suddenly, as they were crossing the lake, a ferocious storm arose, with violent winds and waves that were crashing into the boat until it was nearly swamped. But Jesus was calmly sleeping in the stern, resting on a cushion. So they shook him awake, saying, "Teacher, don't you even care that we are all about to die!" Fully awake, he rebuked the storm and shouted to the sea, "Hush! Be still!" All at once the wind stopped howling and the water became perfectly calm."
Mark 4:37-39 TPT

CHAPTER EIGHTEEN

4-14-22: Prayer Room Results

It's been awhile since I've written anything but God is still working even when I don't see or feel it! This morning around 5am I was awoken with a mandate to pray! I went to our prayer room and started lifting up all those that I felt needed prayer. One of the people that I lifted up was a lady I'll call Sally. I had a brief encounter with her a few days earlier while working on a fence project at our home.

This was a friend of our next door neighbor who we've attempted to reach for Jesus many years. She offered to help with our shared fence but after a few minutes she was unable to continue because of pain in her hands. My husband and I asked to pray for her and she allowed us that pleasure. She apologized for not being able to help on our shared fence but we assured her it was fine and to just take care of herself! We had not seen her or the man next door for over a week so I was concerned for her since I knew he was working out of town.

So I was praying for Sally and then I heard a weird noise outside our home like something pushing against our front door and then loud talking! I cautiously got up and peeked out to see what was happening and I saw what looked like this lady standing in the dark.

I went to tell my husband and he wasn't getting up for this! He's usually the bold one in our home! Mind you I would not have heard this if God had not woken me just twenty minutes earlier! I opened the door slightly and she was standing there in the dark holding a large black comforter while crying profusely.

The crying threw me off since she presented herself previously as a very tough dudette! Her foul language and demeanor did not match what I saw before me in this dark hour of despair. She cried out "can't you see my face?" I said "no but I'll turn on my porch light so I can". When the light came on it revealed a bloody face and hands and sweatpants, that I thought were tie dyed in the dark,but were actually blood spots!

As I saw her standing there clutching the large blanket, I asked her, "What happened?" I asked her to sit down on a chair and I sat across from her while she told me a sad story. She started by saying, through horrendous sobs, I'm going to tell you something but you must not tell anyone. She said, "my stalker has found me again" and "I was raped!"

She looked vulnerable and quite weak unlike the tough gal I had met earlier. My heart broke for her and I proceeded to tell her this was not her fault and that she was a worthy person that is loved by me and Jesus! I told her that she has value! I don't really remember all that I said to her as I was being led by the Spirit at the time.

She responded to me by saying, "thank you for saying that" and "thank you for being there for me". She repeated those words over and over again through her haze of extreme alcohol abuse. She kept saying I feel so gross and dirty and I can't believe this has happened. God gave me the right words to say and the patience to deal with her in her state of mind! He gave me HIS love for her as I hugged her with the comfort that only He can give.

I tried to get her to report this and go to the hospital and she would seem to comply but then changed her mind as soon as I said let's go. I took pictures of her face, hands, and clothes in case she wanted evidence later. She asked me, "will you just do me a favor?" I cautiously said yes. She asked me to take her to a friend's house in the next town where she would be safe. This happened right next door to us! I asked her if he was still in the neighborhood and she was angry and offended at first saying, "now you're worried about the neighborhood?" I said, "No, I'm concerned about you and I!"

Then she calmed down a bit seeing my REAL concern for her. I agreed to take her but she only had the street name but no house number. I drove that way still urging her to report this and we went back and forth several times about this as I drove. She was mostly rambling in her altered state but she began to tell me an amazing story!

She said she was out 150 miles in the ocean and I don't know why or how but she was there. She had this wide-eyed look and said "I saw a dove flying in the sky toward me" and I immediately said "Holy Spirit!". She then replied, "Holy Ghost!" That was the only spiritual thing she said that night but led me to believe that someone had invested in her life at some point.

I tried to take the conversation further but to no avail so then I had to get her attention back on the other task of FINDING the house!

I'm driving this street up and down till she finally pointed out what I hoped was the right place. She was so inebriated that I was leary of her and asked her if she had contact info to let them know she was there. By that time, we were just seeing daylight but we saw no activity. She told me that she would go and sleep in their backyard and there was no stopping her in that decision.

She saw me look at the address on the mailbox and said, "you're checking out the numbers!" I said, "yes because I'm going to check on you later!" The person that raped her also took her phone so I had no other way to follow up.

I went there later that evening with my husband and while he waited for me in the car, I knocked on the door just praying this was the right place. I heard her very loud voice as she answered the door. She was cleaned up on the outside but still in an alcohol induced haze.

I hugged her and told her I loved her. She told me again, in confidence, not to tell anyone, especially her guy friend. She was afraid that the friend might try to kill the guy. She opened up and told me that the person who did the deed was a cop! Now I understood why she kept refusing to go to the police station! She said she was going to handle it "her way" which concerns me but I've given her to Jesus! She told me that she wanted to go to church with me and of course I said anytime! More to come concerning that, I'm sure!

CHAPTER NINETEEN

4-21-22: Prayer Room Update

My husband and I officiated at a Good Friday service out of town the next evening, after my encounter with Sally. We spent the night there after an amazing Holy Spirit move! I shared a short version of this previous story there with discretion of course. The group was smitten with the same love and compassion of God that touched Sally.

The altars were full of hungry people that recognized a faithful God. The message here is, always be obedient and listen to the Lord's calling to pray and then be ready to put into action your love for Him as you love others even in their worst times! His reward is beyond anything you can imagine!

A little side note here. When we returned from our trip I found a small herb in a clay pot outside our front door, right at the same spot where just two days ago Sally stood weeping and hurt! I knew that it was from her although no note was attached. It had been a week since seeing Sally now and I had thought many times to go to that house where I left her to check on her but I kept getting a "no" from the Holy Spirit!

I've been watching out for her and today, a week after the incident, I hear her loud vivacious voice. I went over and immediately gave her a hug and told her that I loved her. I asked if she was the one who left the plant, because I just knew it was her! She replied with "yes" and "I'm so glad you knew it was me!"

I told her, that many times, I wanted to go to that house to check on her. She knew that was the case! She told me that she grew that plant out of one leaf before presenting to me! It had value to her, it represented her attention and love for nature. This was ALL she had to give but it has great value to me!

It was like a child so proud of the dandelions presented to their beloved mommy! It is a Basil plant and she promises to make us an "oldschool", her word for "from scratch", meal when we return next season with all the herbs that she's going to grow. My heart is full and I look forward to more of God's everyday miracles as I follow Him daily! I know this is long but I just obey and He writes!

"Above all, constantly echo God's intense love for one another, for love will be a canopy over a multitude of sins."
1 Peter 4:8 TPT

CHAPTER TWENTY

5-8-22: Changing a Culture

Today was another divine day! The two young brothers, 18 and 15, that I mentioned in a previous chapter, were there and came up for prayer! They had not asked for anything in particular but we're waiting for God to speak into their lives through His humble servant.

I just started telling them about their status as men of God and how amazing they were! I was impressed to encourage them to break a generational curse that invades the Black culture, a fatherless home! They revealed to me that their home has three siblings with three different Dads and none of them were present in their lives! The Holy Spirit knew what needed to be spoken in that moment. They agreed with me that this is very prevalent in their culture.

I told them the same thing that I told my grandson at that age. Be the man that your future Godly wife is looking for!

I addressed gaming with them and I had already addressed sex before marriage when they came up weeks before but the Holy Spirit prompted me to repeat that message of fidelity AFTER marriage as well.

They laughed as I said, "do you think your future spouse wants a guy that plays video games all day?" I knew that the Holy Spirit touched on something there! I told them they needed to stand up and be different then all the other men in their culture! It's ok to be different, in a Godly way! I felt the Holy Spirit's leading to encourage them to be different. It's ok to be peculiar, God says it in His word.

Both of the following Bible versions give a beautiful picture of 1 Peter 2:9. We are peculiar AND we are treasures! We are set apart! Wow!

"But ye are a chosen generation, a royal priesthood, an holy nation, a peculiar people; that ye should shew forth the praises of him who hath called you out of darkness into his marvelous light:"
1 Peter 2:9 KJV

"But you are God's chosen treasure —priests who are kings, a spiritual "nation" set apart as God's devoted ones. He called you out of darkness to experience his marvelous light, and now he claims you as his very own. He did this so that you would broadcast his glorious wonders throughout the world."
1 Peter 2:9 TPT

These young men were longing to be taught the truth. They needed someone to remind them of their value as Godly men! As I spoke those words into their life I'm not sure if they're even saved but God's got their number!

Sometimes we may think that we come across as harsh and to the point, but when it comes to the very life and soul of a person, that thought disappears! They never asked for a specific need, they came up and waited for encouragement, love, wisdom, and whatever else came up.

The key is to LISTEN to the Holy Spirit when you have an encounter and just speak what you hear! It's been an honor to see these young men hungry for more! May we all be MORE hungry and thirsty for God!

"I am the Lord your God, Who brought you out of

the land of Egypt; Open your mouth wide, and I
will fill it."
Psalms 81:10 NKJV

CHAPTER TWENTY-ONE

5-8-22: The Bride

I had this dream in the wee hours of the morning and it actually woke me up. I was wearing a very beautiful traditional white wedding gown with all the lace and big skirts! The dress seems to indicate purity and innocence. I went to a Pub of sorts which is something I never do as I don't partake of alcohol. I met a man there named John and I was hugging him and kissing his cheeks but I didn't have the sense that he was any more than a very treasured friend.

John left the room and left me with a small group of people and when I walked up to them, they said "who are you?" I said, I'm with John. '' They said, "well then come over here and we'll take care of all of your expenses and needs here!" Everyone was laughing and having a good time and then I left to use the bathroom and when I came back everything changed! Everyone that I thought welcomed me, because I was John's friend, was now mocking me and making fun of how they had tricked me into believing that they had accepted me.

Then I woke up and I knew that there was something that the Lord wanted to say to me and others through that dream. The group at the bar represents the world, satan's ways, and how deceiving he can be. Satan's lies will try to deceive us into thinking we can achieve status and acceptance by going his way but the end of that is the death of our spirit.

The attraction of the world can have a strong pull if we are not "attached" to the ultimate source of ALL things good, our Heavenly Father. We need only to be accepted by the very one that created us to be secure and fulfill our destiny here. No person can fulfill what only He can by His consuming love that doesn't judge or condemn but only renews and refreshes!

I believe that the name John has significance through the meaning of the name. The name John comes from the Hebrew language and means "God is gracious". Two highly revered John's were John the Baptist, the forerunner of Jesus, and John the apostle, author of the fourth gospel and Revelation. Both John's were in the inner circle of Jesus and the apostle John was called "the beloved" as he laid his head on Jesus's chest! I want to be in that inner circle as well with my head on His chest and His arms wrapped around me secure, loved, and accepted. Now think again of the picture of the bride of Christ as we present ourselves before Jesus. We have lived a life fully submitted to God even through the mocking of those that hate Him and us as well!

"Let us be glad and rejoice, and let us give honor to him. For the time has come for the wedding feast of the Lamb, and his bride has prepared herself. She has been given the finest of pure white linen to wear." For the fine linen represents the good deeds of God's holy people.
Revelation 19:7-8 NLT

Now reference with this next scripture for the deeds done with wrong motives. The people who do not know God attempt to do things in their own strength with no regard for their creator.

"You welcome those who gladly do good, who follow godly ways. But you have been very angry with us, for we are not godly. We are constant sinners; how can people like us be saved? We are all infected and impure with sin. When we display our righteous deeds, they are nothing but filthy rags. Like autumn leaves, we wither and fall, and our sins sweep us away like the wind."

Isaiah 64:5-6 NLT

So which garment will we choose, the Bridal garment or the filthy rags? And which materials will we use for our foundation, gold, silver, jewels or wood, hay, or straw? It is possible to build on the true foundation of Christ BUT with the wrong materials! God wants us to do this His way with materials that will last through the fire!

"For no one can lay any foundation other than the one we already have—Jesus Christ. Anyone who builds on that foundation may use a variety of materials—gold, silver, jewels, wood, hay, or straw. But on the judgment day, fire will reveal what kind of work each builder has done. The fire will show if a person's work has any value."
1 Corinthians 3:11-13 NLT

"If the work survives, that builder will receive a reward. But if the work is burned up, the builder will suffer great loss. The builder will be saved, but like someone barely escaping through a wall of flames."
1 Corinthians 3:14-15 NLT

I want to be like brother Abraham who looked for a heavenly city!

"His eyes of faith were set on the city with unshakable foundations, whose architect and builder is God himself."

Hebrews 11:10 TPT

When we apply God's building plans to our lives through faith we inherit ALL that He has made available to us! We need to choose our garments, those of praise, wedding, and armor, as well as our foundational materials of gold, silver and jewels in order to line with His destiny for our lives!

9-23-22

Here I am months later and I've put off actually getting this piece ready to publish, somewhat out of fear of failure but mostly because I have forgotten some of the processes to get through to completion! I've prayed, listened to YouTube videos, called around to find some help, prayed more, and then I sat down and asked the Holy Spirit to teach me! Well this has been interesting! He began to reveal to me each step but not until I put faith into action to try! I've had so much peace even though I've done each step over and over again. I'm talking like 15 times! He's making sure I've got it. He is so faithful to His promises and will never fail me when I ask Him for help!

I am certain that God who has begun the good

work within you, will continue His work until it is finally finished on the day when Christ Jesus returns. Phil. 1:6 NLT

Dedication

I want to give credit to the Holy Spirit for all His help on this book. This has been quite a journey of faith for me and He has not failed to prove Himself powerful on my behalf!

Other books by Debrah J Smith

Pearls of Wisdom
ISBN-9798642460764

Grandma's Clothesline
ISBN-97819546266003

Made in the USA
Middletown, DE
07 October 2022

12108402R10046